Fingerpower® Transposer

Level One

Melodic Technic Exercises with Integrated Transposing

by Wesley Schaum

Foreword

This unique series integrates the benefits of Fingerpower exercises with .... Transposing helps develop ear training and awareness of melodic contour. At Level One, key signatures are introduced and expanded to include D Major and B-flat Major in both treble and bass staffs.

These exercises present simple melodic and harmonic intervals. The student learns to recognize these intervals on the printed page, hear the different sounds, and also experience the feeling in the hand as various intervals are played.

Each exercise has melodic elements delineated by phrase marks. Students are taught to recognize phrase groups that recur in the same piece. This process helps in learning and memorizing these exercises. Awareness of phrase groups also helps to enhance music reading skills beyond this book.

EXCLUSIVELY DISTRIBUTED BY

HAL•LEONARD®

1. Broken and Blocked 3rds – C Position

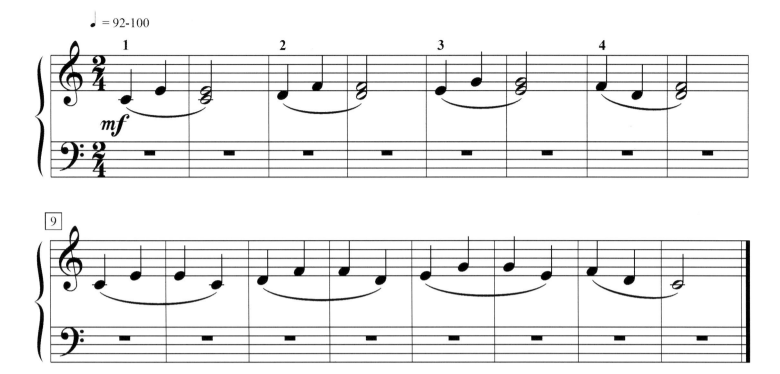

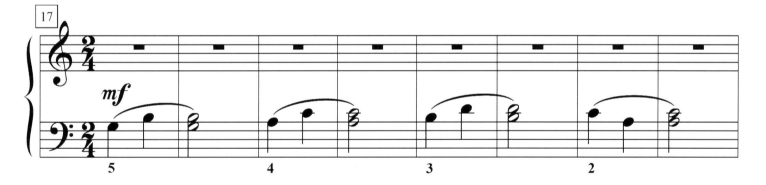

Transposed to G Position:

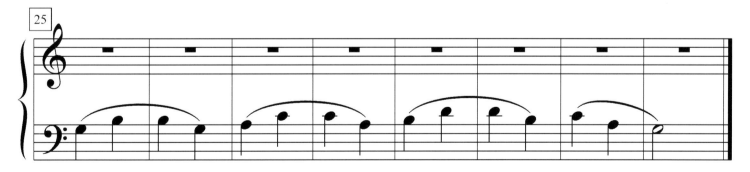

2. Blocked 3rds – F Position

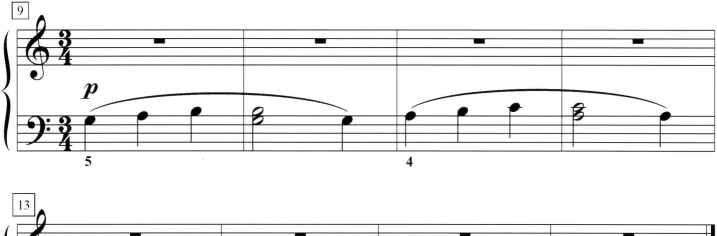

Transposed to G Position:

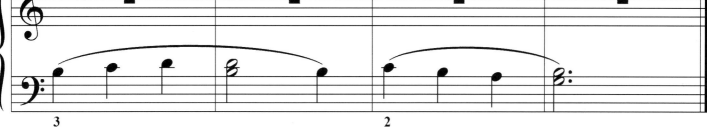

3. Blocked and Broken 4ths – F Position

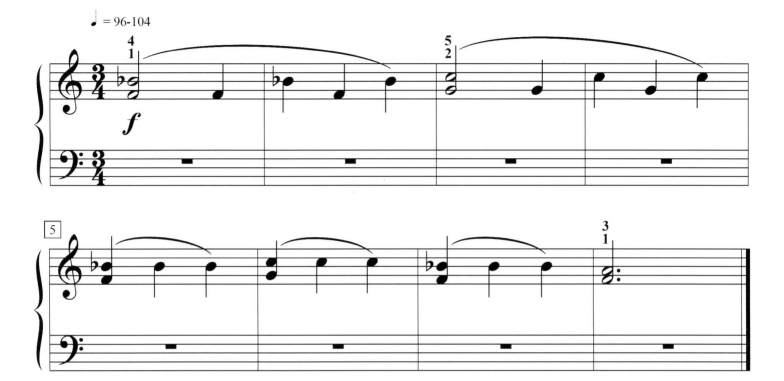

Transposed to C Position:

4. Blocked 4ths – Left Hand F Position

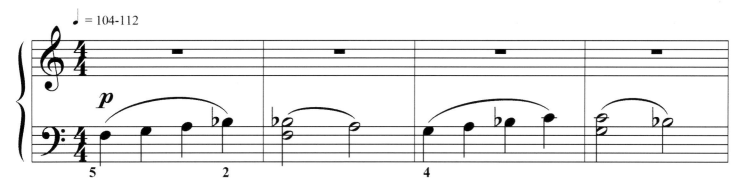

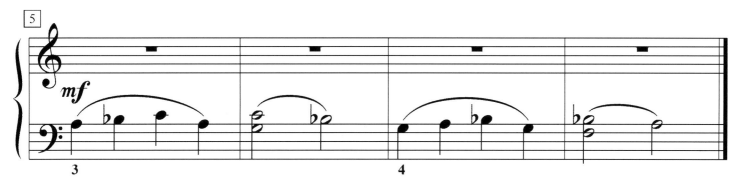

Right Hand F Position:

Teacher's Note: Point out that the Left Hand F Position is ***one octave lower*** than the Right Hand F Position.

5. 3rds and 4ths – Right Hand C Position

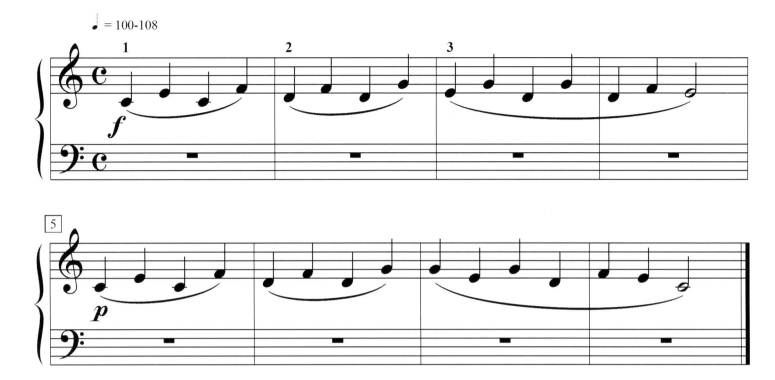

Left Hand C Position:

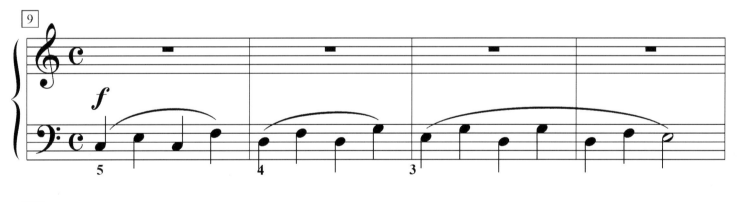

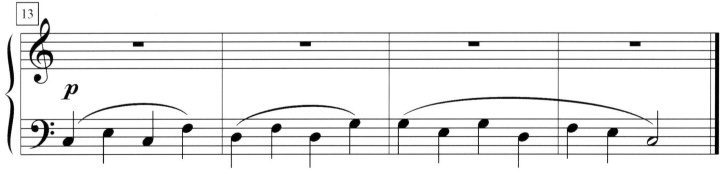

6. Melody with Accompaniment for L.H. and R.H.

Transposed to C Major:

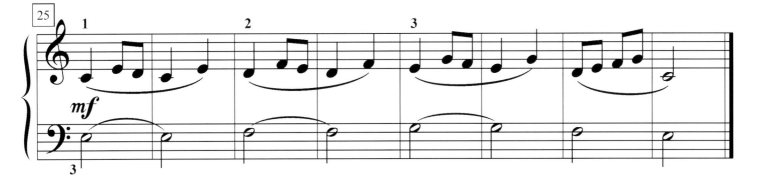

7. Broken and Blocked 2nds – C Position

Transposed to G Position:

8. Right Hand Melody – C Position

Transposed to G Position:

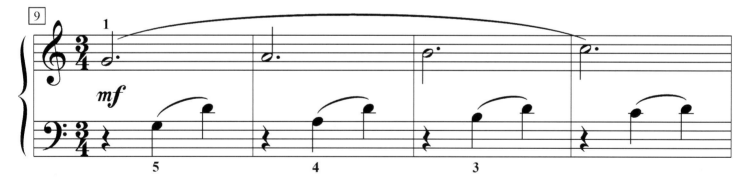

9. 3rds with 8th Notes and Staccato

Transposed to F Position:

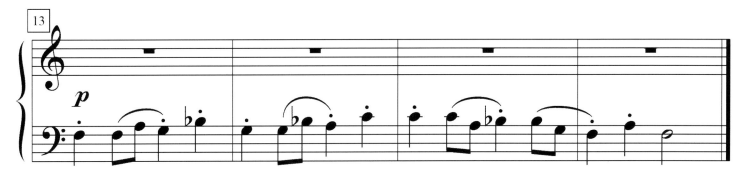

10. Groups of Four 8th Notes – G Position

Transposed to C Position:

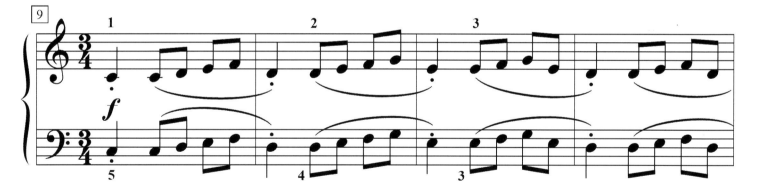

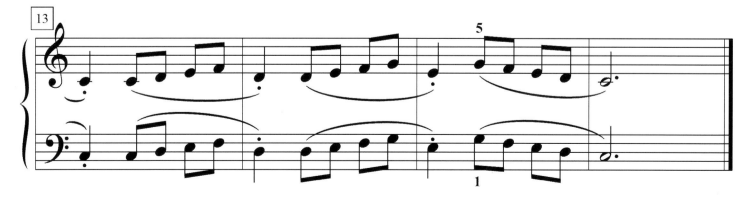

11. G Major Melody with Key Signature

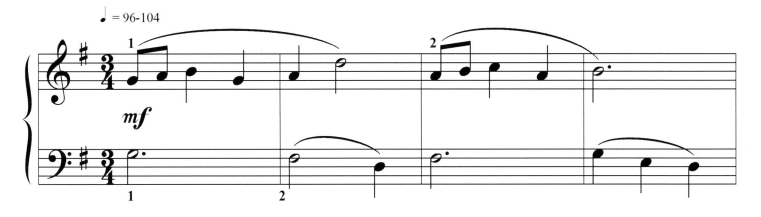

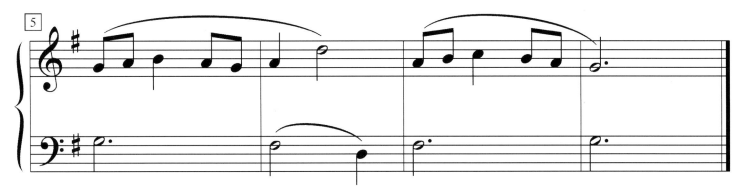

Transposed to C Major:

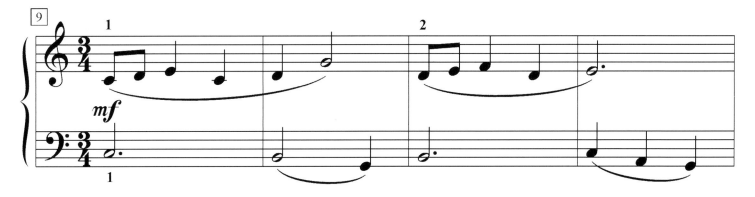

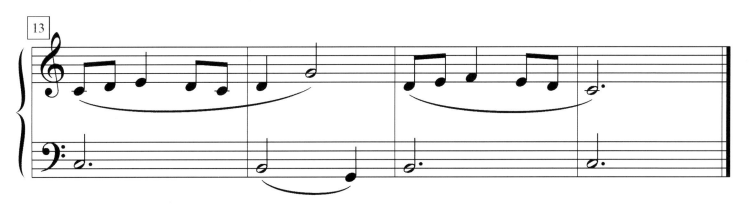

12. Melody Divided Between the Hands

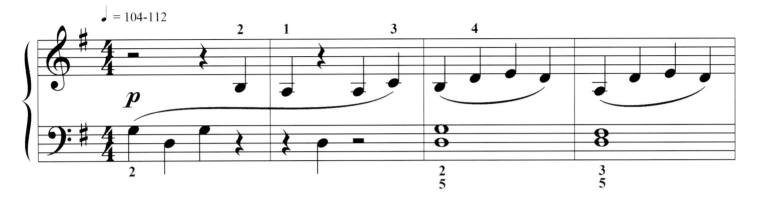

Transposed to C Major:

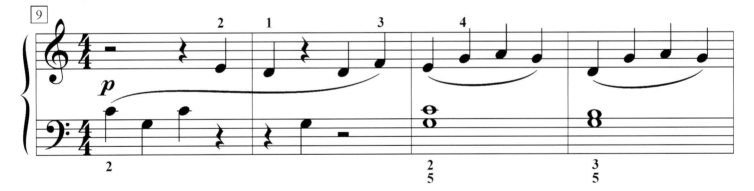

13. F Major Melody for R.H. with Key Signature

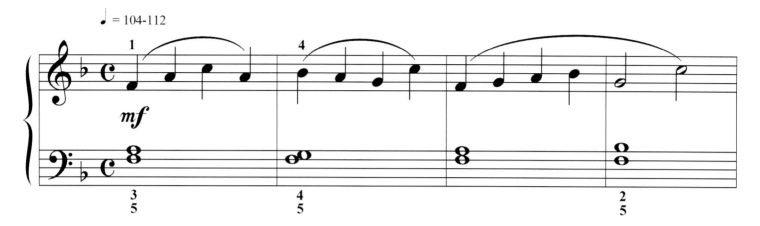

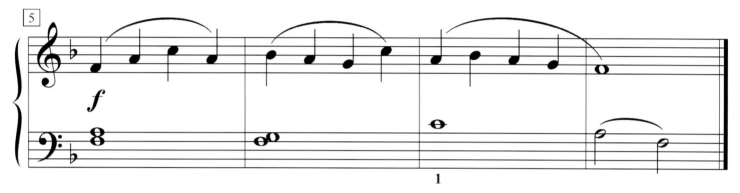

Left Hand F Major Melody:

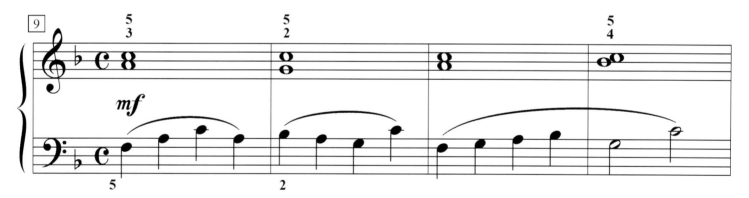

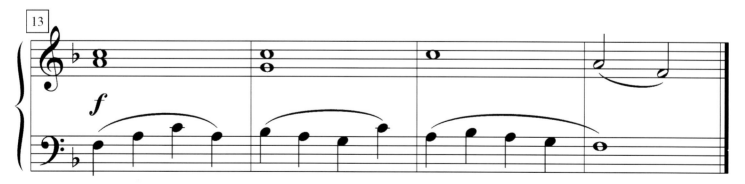

Teacher's Note: The whole note accompaniments are purposely different in each of the hand positions.

14. F Major Melody Alternating Between Hands

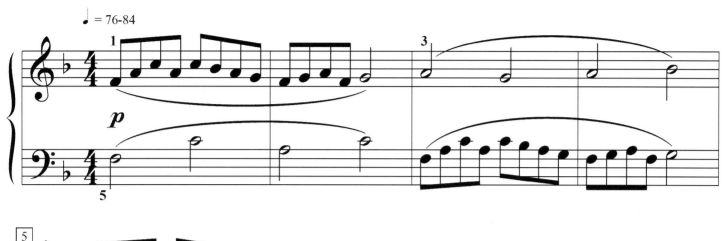

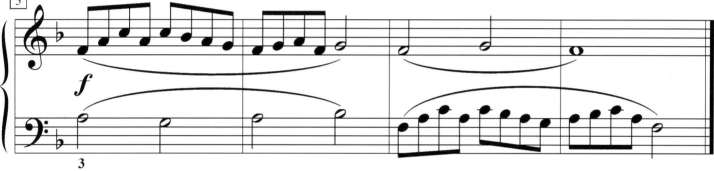

Transposed to G Major:

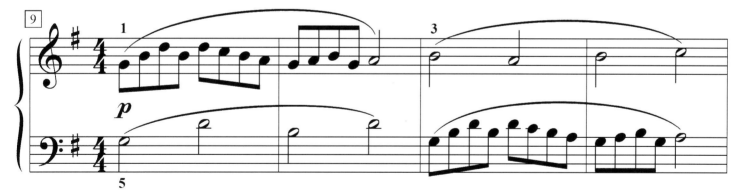

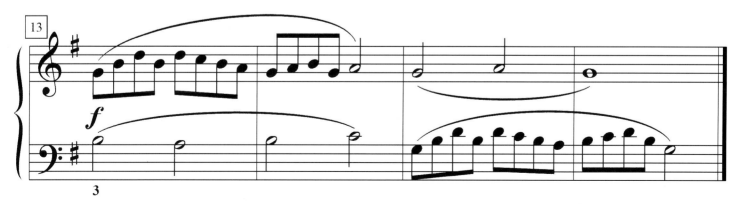

15. D Major Melody for R.H. with Key Signature

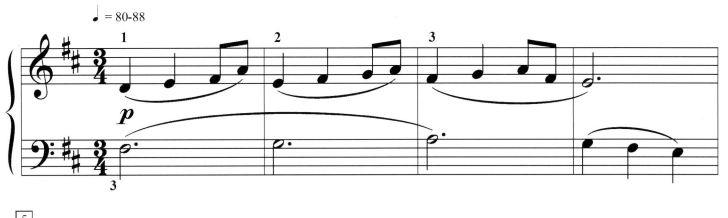

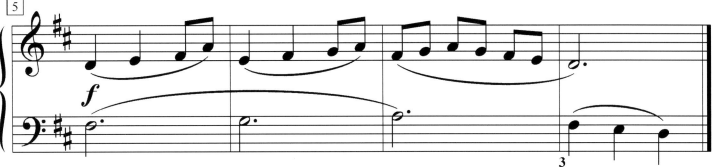

Left Hand D Major Melody:

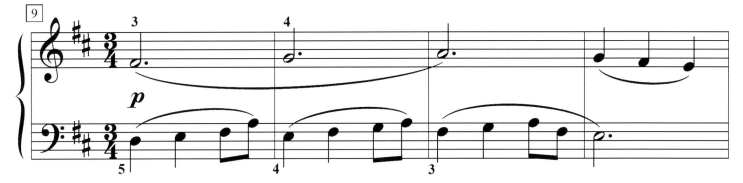

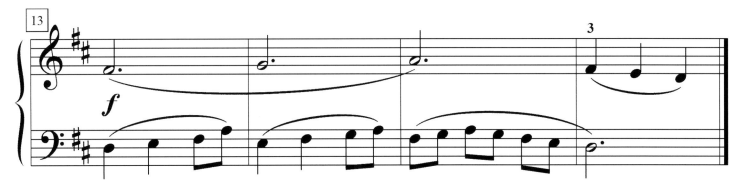

16. D Major 5-Finger Pattern

Transposed to C Major:

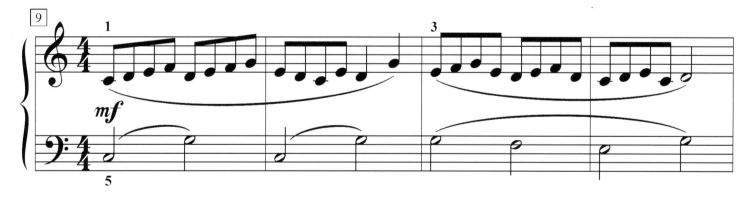

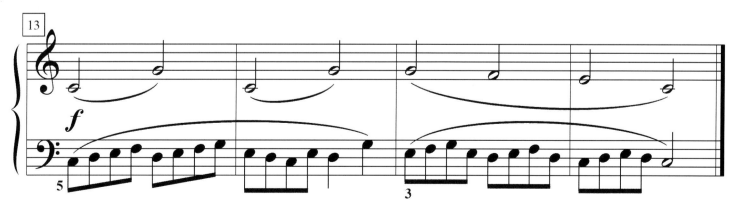

18

17. B-flat Pattern for R.H. with Key Signature

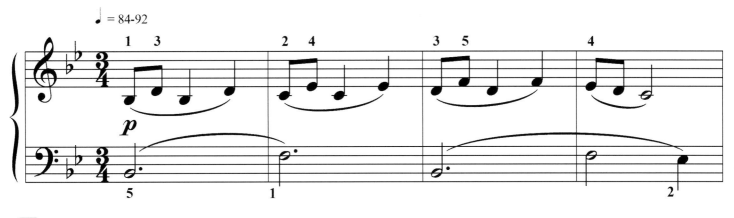

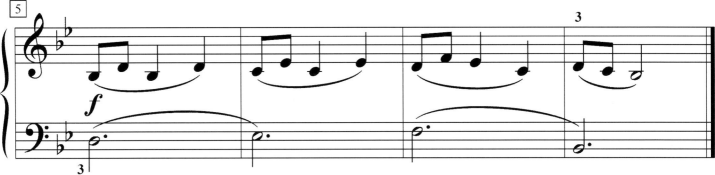

Left Hand B-flat Pattern:

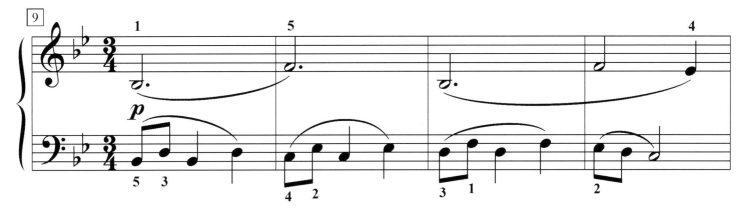

18. Parallel and Contrary Motion in D Major

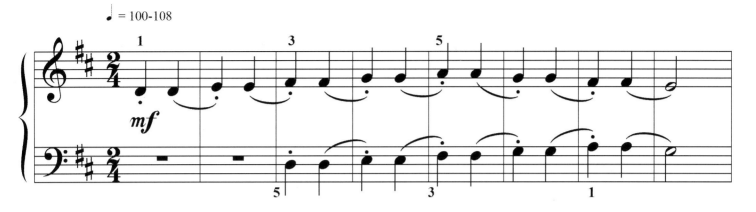

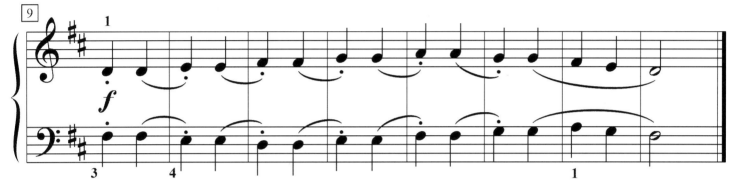

Transposed to F Major:

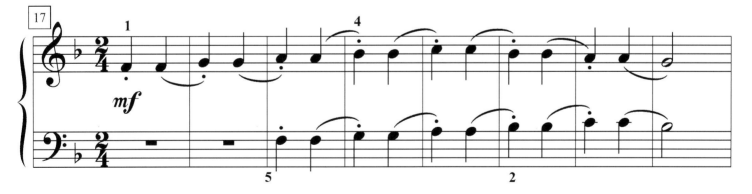

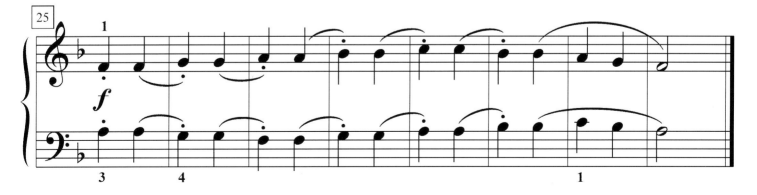

19. Staccato Pattern in B-flat Major

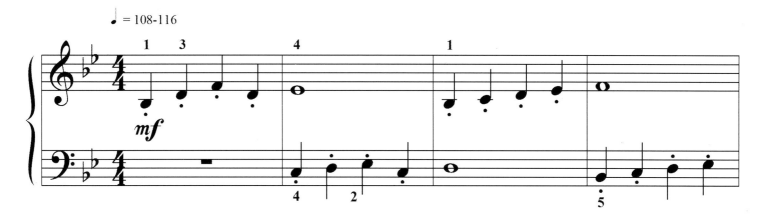

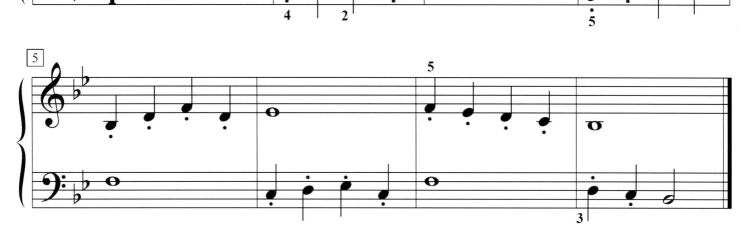

Transposed to D Major:

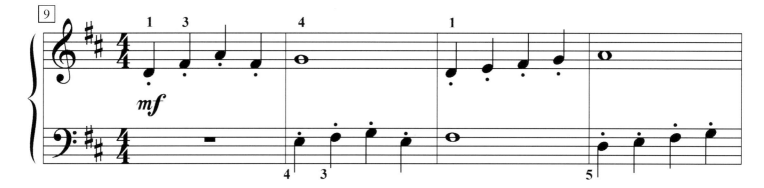

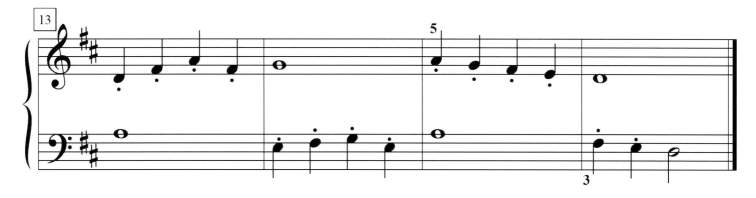

20. B-flat Major 5-Finger Pattern

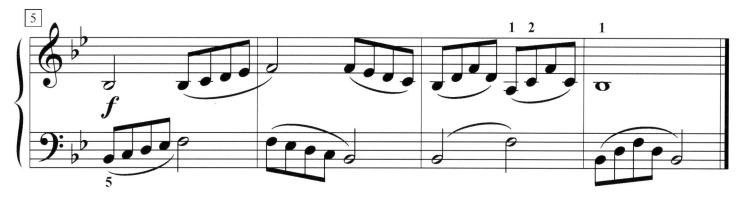

Transposed to G Major:

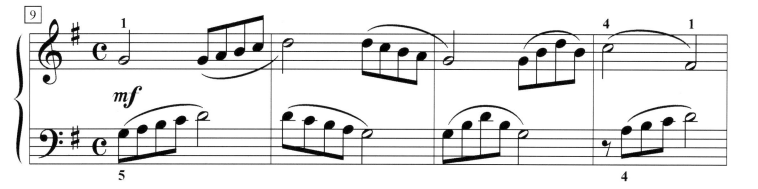

21. F Major Melody with 1st/2nd Endings

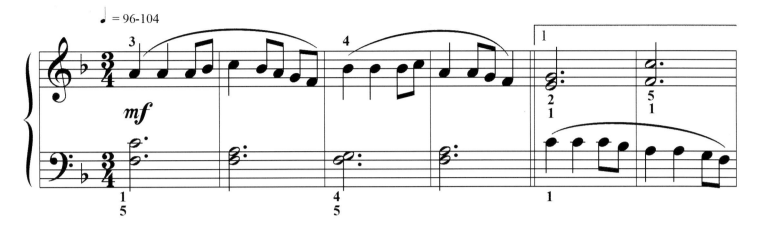

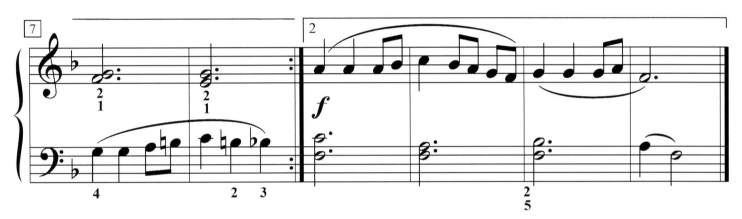

Transposed to G Major:

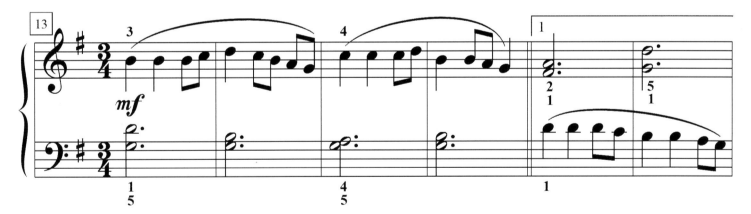

Teacher's Note: First and second endings may have to be explained to the student.

Transposed to B-flat Major:

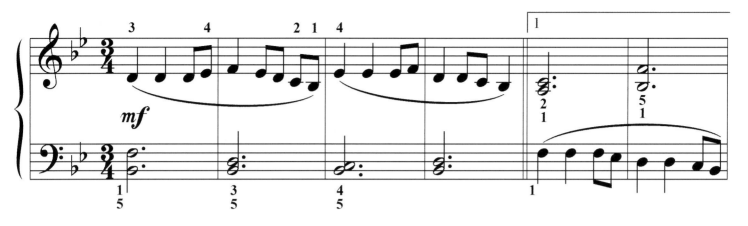

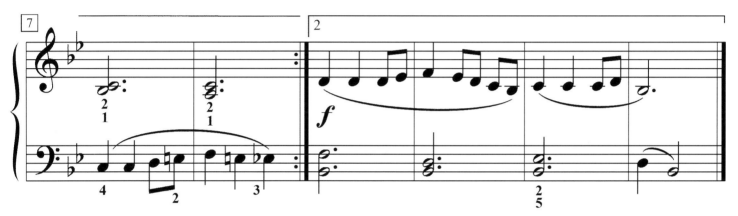

Transposed to D Major:

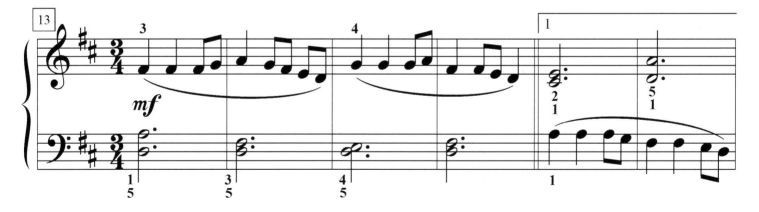

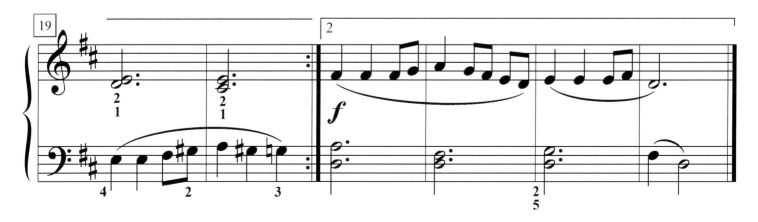